CAUTIONS TO YOUNG SPORTSMEN

CAUTIONS TO YOUNG SPORTSMEN

BY

SIR THOMAS FRANKLAND, BART.,

SECOND EDITION 1801

**Republished 1985 with New Introductory Material
© by W. S. Curtis**

Published by
W. S. CURTIS (Publishers)

Printed by Kopy Kraft of Bedford.

ISBN 0-948216-04-2

INTRODUCTION

The end of the 18th Century was a time of increasing use of the sporting gun. The advent of Nock's Patent Breech in 1787 together with improvements in the quality of gunpowder had shortened and lightened barrels enabling the double barrel to become ever more common and wing shooting or, as it was known, "Shooting Flying" became fashionable.

Matching the interest in the gunroom was the interest in the library catered for by such authors as Thomas Page whose *ART OF SHOOTING FLYING* appeared in at least six editions between 1766 and 1782. The celebrated *ESSAY ON SHOOTING* of 1789 produced anonymously by William Cleator was published in large numbers to judge by the surviving specimens and formed the groundwork for many later volumes and in particular the shooting sections of the large sporting encyclopædias popular at the time.

No one, however, had seriously contemplated the subject of safe gun handling and shooting accidents, which were even then exacting a tragic toll, until in 1800 Sir Thomas Frankland produced *CAUTIONS TO YOUNG SPORTSMEN*, which concentrated on this aspect although adequately handling the general management of the sporting gun. The successful reception of the book led to the publication of an enlarged second edition in 1801 which is the original of this facsimile reproduction.

The numerous anecdotes recounted in the book were used by other authors almost immediately, indeed the Rev'd W.B.Daniel did so in *RURAL SPORTS* in 1801 stating (Vol.II, p.105) that Frankland's material is used "...in the full persuasion that he wishes the *HINTS* he has drawn up should be as universally imparted as possible."

Sir Thomas Frankland was the sixth Baronet from the original creation of 1660 inheriting both the baronetcy and the estates of Thirkleby from his father, a Vice Admiral of the Red, on 21st November 1784. On succeeding his father he caused the old Elizabethan Hall to be demolished and constructed a new mansion on higher ground to the North from designs by Wyatt. Thirkleby itself lies in North Yorkshire not far from the Great North Road and about ten miles East North East of Ripon in an area most suited to field sports.

Sir Thomas was born on 18th September 1750 and educated at Eton, Oxford (Merton) and Lincoln's Inn acquiring his M.A. in 1771. He represented nearby Thirsk in Parliament from 1774 to 1780 and again from 1796 to 1801 where he consistently voted for the opposition following the examples of his father and his uncle who had sat for Thirsk from 1768 to 1774. In 1792 he was High Sheriff of Yorkshire. His son and heir Robert was born in 1784 and succeeded to the title at the death of Sir Thomas on 4th January 1831. Sir Robert died in 1849 without male offspring and was succeeded in the Thirkleby estate by his daughter Emily Anne the mother of Sir Ralph Payne-Gallwey the noted late 19th Century author of such well known shooting books as *THE FOWLER IN IRELAND* (1882), *THE BOOK OF DUCK DECOYS* (1886) and the series of *LETTERS TO YOUNG SHOOTERS* (1890 to 1896). Thirkleby became the residence of Sir Ralph who chronicled the family history and who had Frankland as a middle name.

The 18th Century saw a flowering of the last of those truly all round intellects with the money and the leisure to cultivate a wide variety of tastes and to become extraordinarily competent at whatsoever undertaking was attempted. Sir Thomas Frankland has been described as an author, artist, scientist, mechanician, classical scholar, botanist, florist, naturalist and authority on British sports. Yet if it was not for this work and for the biographical notes of his great grandson Payne-Gallwey he would be completely forgotten today. In presenting this little book the compiler hopes that it will provide both pleasure and instruction to the present day generation of collectors of books and guns and to the practical flintlock shotgunner.

The compiler acknowledges with gratitude the research assistance rendered by Christopher Smith of the Bedfordshire County Library.

W.S.Curtis 18th June 1985

Bibliography References- Riling No. 330,
                              Gerrare No. 402
                              Schwerdt Vol I. P. 187

CAUTIONS

TO

YOUNG SPORTSMEN.

[PRICE ONE SHILLING.]

Cautions

TO

YOUNG SPORTSMEN.

BY

SIR THOMAS FRANKLAND, BART.

FACIENT ALIENA PERICULA CAUTUM.

The Second Edition with Additions.

London:
sold by
JAMES ROBSON, NEW BOND STREET.

J. SMEETON, PRINTER, ST. MARTIN'S LANE.

1801.

ADVERTISEMENT

TO THE

SECOND EDITION.

From the form in which these few pages first appeared, it must have been evident that extensive circulation, with a view to prevent those evils which every Sportsman has it in his own power to avoid, was their only object.

Had any thing on the subject been already before the Public, a then recent event, which plunged families of Rank into deep affliction, would have been an excuse for a re-publication, which might rouse Shooters to a sense of their danger; but I knew of few Cautions in print beyond the vague words in Page's "Art of Shooting Flying", *Be careful, yet not timorous.*[1] There are indeed numerous warnings

---

[1] To bid a Man keep his Temper when he Shoots ill, is advice nearly as unprofitable; but I shall venture to recommend that he may not dash his gun from him, when put a little out of sorts by

warnings to be derived from the scattered relations in newspapers; in which we read of one young lad having his arm shattered by firing an un-measured charge from a cankered and honeycombed barrel; of another dragging his gun, by the muzzle, pointed at his own head, through a thick hedge; and other similar effects of barbarous ignorance; but there appeared a want of such regular advice as might be attended to by those who are supposed to be better instructed.

If this attempt at instilling more systematic care can be promoted in one tittle by its being openly acknowledged by an old sportsman, in compliance

---

by missing, as I fear is sometimes practised, without much mending the matter. Still less let him imitate a frolic of the late Marquis of Granby, on the Moors at BUMPER HALL, (his Sporting box, not uncharacteristically named,) who, on his flint, in a windy day, having repeatedly missed fire, bestowing some hearty compliments on his attendant, and gun, grasped the butt with both hands, and swinging the muzzle round, struck it against a large stone with such force as (to use the expression of the relator, an eye witness now living) bent the barrel into the form of a *sickle*.

with

with the opinion of my Friends, I here readily throw in the mite of declaring myself. My conduct as an Author is indeed still incompleat, for, according to modern fashion, I ought to exhibit my own portrait as a frontispiece,—beautifully engraved,—in a Shooting Jacket.[a]

Since this letter first made its appearance, a variety of accidents have been related to me; all of them referable to some head of danger which I have pointed out, but mostly occasioned by the mistaken practice of cocking Guns unnecessarily soon. This usage cannot have arisen from an apprehension of the wanting time, or strength, but from a doubt whether the operation might not be totally forgotten on the emergency. If after a rea-

---

[a] On seeing suits of Armour in old Halls, I have often thought they would make an excellent dress for Shooting in strong Cover, and recommend it to some stouter Man than myself to try the experiment. It would at least have a good effect in terrifying Poachers, till the contents of the Lion's skin should be found out. Had I thus caparisoned myself at the head of my book, I might at first sight have actually passed for a Hero.

sonable number of years practice a man should still be so put off his guard on the rising of a Jack-snipe,[3] that

[3] However the Man of skill may quizz the humble Shooter, whom one Jack-snipe lasts for a Season, I shall inform him that two noted Keepers shot twelve times at one, in Windsor Forest, and *left him marked;* as one of them (mentioned in note 11,) informed me. The other was remarkable for using a long gun in cover, for which he gave this notable reason, that a long gun would kill at a short distance, but a short gun would not kill at a long distance.

Notwithstanding the facility with which Snipes are missed, I have known Ladies propose the knocking down a few for a corner dish, as if it were cracking so many nuts; and naturally enough, for they hear of Game finding its way into the larder;* but however

* The following is a simple method of *dating* the day on which birds were killed. Let the six fore toes, represent the six shooting days of the week. The left toe of the left foot answering for Monday, count from thence to the right toe of the right foot, which is to pass for Saturday. Let any portion of that toe which corresponds to the day on which the bird was killed be cut off. If a part of one or more toes has been shot off, cut that which is to register the day still shorter. I am aware that a whole foot may be carried away, but in general the practice will answer. Perhaps in a well regulated Larder, what I propose may be idle, but it is particularly useful in the case of Game sent *weekly* from distant Manors.

that he should not recollect the construction of a gun lock, I would seriously advise him, if he continues to think himself cut out for a Sportsman, to adopt some other pursuit in the field; notwithstanding

ever they may know that Woodcocks are not shot sitting on trees, or Pheasants swimming, are ignorant of the almost military fatigue† with which they are frequently procured; not to mention *Skill*, of which those who know the least make the lightest.

The late Mr. Scroggs, an excellent marksman, enticed into the field such a sort of burly-wigged character, as is represented in the well known print of Jollux; who had heard of Shooting, and was willing for once to see what it was like. The Doctor followed very gallantly;—crossed several hedges, (not without suffering a rent in his lower garments,) and seeing eight or ten birds killed in succession considered the thing as an absolute Q. E. D. At length came an unfair shot, and a miss;—this was a *quod est absurdum* most unexpected; *Oh, fie, fie, Mr. Scroggs, how could you tell me you was a good* SHOTSMAN!

† Hunger and thirst, shattered nerves, sweltering heat, and drenching rain, are more peculiarly the lot of the Grouse Shooter. But the Leicestershire Hunter will plead that his toils (and no doubt his joys,) are still greater; and will tell me, that the spirited stile in which he risks his neck, at every fence, has set such an example to the British Cavalry, that had they been at the battle of *Marengo*, they would have taken the famous ditch at a Canter.

withstanding that some of his wag friends may define Angling to be *a stick and a string, with a Worm at one end, and a Fool at the other,* and that he may find *Diachylon* an expensive article on having rode a mile or two extraordinary. I knew a Gentleman some years ago, who wished to amuse himself with practical Mechanics, but confessed to me that he never could see *the shape of a piece of hot iron.* How far he might have succeeded as a Cobler I know not, but I dissuaded him from turning Smith. Had he however persisted in either line, *invitâ Minervâ,* and the goddess had directed the pricking, or even burning, of his fingers, slight would have been the evil, in comparison to what that Sportsman hazards, who is so agitated at the rising of a partridge, that he cannot "discern the form thereof;" and to disqualify himself still further, like Gil Blas attacking with the robbers, shuts both his eyes on drawing the trigger.

As I have fortunately seldom seen Wild Beasts, except at the Tower, or at Exeter Change, I cannot positively judge how far I might be master of my Gun-lock, and of my wits, if I should *Soho* a
great

great Lion, with his saucer eyes glaring at me through a bush; but it appears that Messrs. Thunberg, Mason, and Co. in a botanical excursion from the Cape, having heard of some Drawcansir Beast, so mistrusted their nerves, that they *rode the whole day with their guns ready Cocked.* (Thunberg's Travels, Vol. 2, Page 149.) Query, Whether their anxiety at setting out in the morning, might not have endangered their forgetting this precaution, which would have been more compleat if all the guns had been *Cocked over Night!* the mainsprings would at least have become more mellow.

Sportsmen are as unwilling to be instructed as others. One may bid me teach my Granny; another offer to shoot with me for a hundred; but the question of *Danger* remains the same. However we may calculate from *probabilities*, a proper attention to the muzzle prevents the *possibility* of mischief from one source. When a Keeper of the Earl of Chesterfield's, (in Thorney-wood Chace, near Nottingham,) was preparing for the field, in Jan. 1789, and stooping to buckle on his spur—as he sat with his gun resting on his knee, and the muzzle close to his cheek,—it seemed *improbable that a part of the lock should break* at that particular point of time; but his instantaneous death was the horrible effect of his not having guarded against what was *possible!*

For what I have left unsaid, or have ill said on the subject, let me be justified by my intentions. I must not flatter myself that one double-barrelled gun will be laid aside, from any suggestion of mine, but if they should be used with greater caution, and I should be so fortunate as to save one pang to the Friends of a hitherto careless Shooter, I shall set it down as A GOOD DAY'S SPORT.

THE writer of the following Letter might perhaps have made it more impressive, if he had collected into one view a number of the accidents which have happened from the ignorance, or negligence, of those who take Guns in hand; but he fears that any deficiency on this melancholy head will be but too readily supplied by most of his readers!

He has introduced the *name* of only one person,[4] and that for

---

[4] He has been advised to deviate in some degree from this his first resolution.

the purpose of recording the good judgment of a keen and high-spirited sportsman, whose apprehensions have since been fatally justified in several inftances. One of the few accidents alluded to, which relates to the blowing up of a powder-flask, in the act of loading, points out a source of danger seldom taken into consideration.

CAUTIONS

CAUTIONS

TO

YOUNG SPORTSMEN.

Dear Sir,

In answer to your questions on the subject of SHOOTING, and particularly referring yourself to my opinion on *double-barrelled Guns*, I shall endeavour to give you such hints as my experience may render of any service to you.

Whether a sportsman who has the perfect management of a *double* Gun can kill more game with it in a season, than he, or another person, *cæteris paribus*, can with a *single*, is not here the question; but whether the many circumstances of inconvenience, and danger, attending the *double*, do not overballance

overballance the advantages, admitted to their fullest extent; and whether upon the whole it is desirable for a young, or indeed any sportsman to use one[5].

You are aware that we adopted the double Gun from the French; among whom the few who, under the old government, had the liberty of shooting, frequently got more shots in one day than you do in a month[6]. From the abundance of game they had the opportunity of picking their shots, which

[5] To an advocate for the double gun, I need not point out its advantages; and he will be satisfied in my admitting its superiority whenever shots are very earnestly required. This however *he* will apply to every case; *I* only to the destruction of vermin, and for defence;—(unhappily too much confided in for this latter purpose by the immortal COOK!) My own experience has proved it a very useful tool, when those sworn friends, a Lurcher and Cur, have made a party of pleasure together into preserved grounds.

[6] In those days when a Poacher in France might be *envoyé un petit peu aux* GALERES, Arthur Young thus described the quantity of game, in the open fields about Montgeron. " There is on an average a covey of birds in every two acres, besides favorite spots,

which made very small charges answer their purpose; besides that, their shoulders could not have supported such as we find more effectual. The smallness of the charge required admitted of the French Guns being made so slight that many

persons

spots, in which they abound much more." (See Young's French Tour, A. D. 1787, &c.)‡

I am assured that on the last day, which the unfortunate Louis XV. enjoyed in the field, he himself shot 572 head of game in eight hours. But as a record of slaughtered game, I shall mention the Engraved " Table d'une Chasse, &c." now before me, which registers the feats of a party from Vienna, in the Bohemian territories, A. D. 1753. It contains columns specifying twenty days, (beginning Aug. 29;) names of the 23 Sports*men* and *Women*; their Shots each day; with the number and kinds of Game killed, (beginning Stags, Roebucks, Boars, Foxes, &c.) The Emperor himself had the greatest number of Shots, viz. 9794, of which 978 were in one day. S. A. R. la Princesse Charlotte was in the field every day; on one of which she fired 889 times. Total of Shots 116,231, Game killed 47,950.

Most

‡ It may not be amiss to observe that a few Sportsmen in this Country, as an encouragement for Farmers to give the Game fair play, have lately established a regular fee for every head killed, payable to the Tenant of the Soil.

persons in this country have supposed their Iron of a quality superior to ours; but many of them have been burst here with very moderate charges. I shall mention one instance of their extreme thinness—that I had once a double Gun, from the reputed best maker in Paris, in which the pattern of the ornaments chased on each side of the sight were distinctly seen, indented, on looking through the barrels. Because the French Guns are usually made too slight for our purpose, it does not follow that we cannot make them safe; but the fact is, that from fear of over weight, and of the breech being made so wide that the left cock should be reached with

Most of the shooting anecdotes relate to the *Skill* and *Success*. I shall here present my readers with one in which there was little of either, but abundant *Sport*,—as I heard it related, more than once, by the late Lt. Col. Walter Strickland in 1784. On the day before one of the annual parties at Clumber broke up, two sets went out, each consisting of three persons; and a bet was laid which should kill most game. It was computed that on an average each man got sixty shots; total=360. The winning triumvirate killed three birds! The shooters were Ld. Lincoln, Gen[l]. Philips, Capt. (afterwards Gen[l].) Lascelles, Rev. Mr. Lascelles, Mr. Cotton, and Lt. Col. Strickland.

difficulty,

difficulty, we have made them so slight that I am sorry to say I could furnish you with a well attested catalogue of double Guns, of English make, burst within these few years, attended with various injuries. It must however be acknowledged that the objection of the locks being too far separated is entirely removed by one of the patents now in force[7], by which the utmost strength required may be introduced at the breech.

That you may not suppose I recommend high loading, I must explain myself more fully, by observing that if a man expects to get fifteen or twenty shots in a day, it will be of no advantage to him to use such a charge as would be more agreeable to his shoulder in case he should get two hundred; and that an ounce and three quarters, or seven eights, of shot will tell better in the field than the Frenchman's charge-meagre of one ounce. Two ounces of shot is the charge proposed in Page's ingenious treatise on " Shooting Flying;" you will therefore hardly think that my

---

[7] Joseph Manton's, of Davies Street.

using

using one ounce and three quarters can class me with those shooters against whom the following severe restriction was levelled, at the foot of an advertisement for pigeon shooting, at Billingbear Warren-house,—*N. B. No person to be allowed to load with more than* FOUR *ounces of shot!*—A gamekeeper, to whom I mentioned this, laughed, and said he thought it *pretty fair allowance.* On my asking him what weight of shot he himself used, he answered that he divided *one pound into five charges.*

A friend of mine seeing his keeper equipping himself for a pigeon match, was curious to examine the terrors of the prepared charge, and trying it with the rammer, expressed his surprize at finding it rather *less* than usual. *Oh! Sir*, replied the keeper, *I have only put in the* POWDER *yet*.

Of this school are the wild-fowl shooters; in one of whose guns, of six feet barrel, I lately measured a charge to the height of *eleven fingers.*—*Sir, I likes to give my Gun a belly-ful.*

He

He who gives a double gun the greatest advantage has both locks cocked when he prepares to shoot, and discharges each barrel in succession, either at separate objects, or the same, as circumstances may require, without removing the butt from his shoulder. Should only one trigger be drawn, there remains one lock cocked; and though there *may* be shooters who have never once omitted to let down the unused cock to the half-bent, I appeal to numbers whether they have not, at some time or other, detected themselves in having loaded one barrel while the lock of that which remained undischarged was still cocked![8] On making this discovery, in his own case, the late Sir George Armytage immediately laid aside his double gun, and soon afterwards gave it to a friend,[9] who, having both locks

---

[8] So many confessions have been made to me on this head of danger, that I cannot set it before the rising generation of Sportsmen in too strong a light.

[9] Matthew Dodsworth, Esq. of Crake Hill near Bedale.

cocked, and being unused to two triggers, inadvertently drew that of the left lock, by which his waistcoat and shirt were set on fire, and his skin burnt. This ill-fated gun was then consigned to a servant, in whose hands it afterwards burst.

Though there may be some advantage in having both locks cocked, it is very practicable to take the Gun down from the shoulder, on having missed a bird with the first barrel, cock, and kill the same bird with the second barrel.[10]

If both locks are cocked it is usual to pull the hinder trigger first. If the forward trigger is drawn first, there is a risk of the finger slipping over it when it gives way, and touching that behind. Whether this sometimes happens,

---

[10] This is particularly suited to shooting in cover, where an unfair shot is often taken, at a short distance, as the best that seems likely to be got, and the Game afterwards passes into open view, so that the single gun shooter regrets his not having a second barrel.

or

or one is shaken off by the recoil, or the sears are made so long as to touch one another, it is certain that both barrels are sometimes unintentionally discharged by one pull. I was witness to this happening in the hands of a late keeper, in Berkshire,[11] who twice, in succession, fired both barrels at once at woodcocks. I was at the edge of the cover, and could just perceive an interval between the sound of the two explosions. On taxing him with the fact he acknowledged it; but could give no account how it had

---

[11] Anthony Griffin, of Billingbear; whose successor informs me that he himself has witnessed the accident repeatedly, from the same gun, in the same hands; and that he particularly remembers its happening *three times* in one day.

The following extraordinary circumstances were related to me by Sir. John Sebright, Bart. who was aiming across a strong wind, when his leeward lock missed fire; the other trigger being immediately drawn, the windward priming, inflamed, communicated across the breech to the leeward pan, and both barrels went off at once! The same effect was also produced on the succeeding shot, which was aimed in the same direction.

happened;

happened; and seemed well satisfied on producing his two birds,—most compleatly peppered.

If only one lock is cocked, the wrong trigger may be drawn; and not answering the pull, whatever part of the work is weakest may be strained, or even broke.[12]

[12] To obviate this the *Double Sear* was invented; but the force of the mainspring, at half bent, being thus resisted by only one half of the usual breadth of sear, it was justly considered as unsafe, and soon laid aside. Notwithstanding the inconvenience of *two* triggers, I must give them the preference to the contrivance of having *one* to suit both locks. I have seen the single trigger made on two constructions; in each of which it answers either lock which is cocked alone; but if both are cocked, in one case, the trigger draws them both off at once; in the other, one particular barrel is necessarily fired by a first pull, and the trigger returning to its place, by a spring, a second pull fires the remaining charge. To this I must object that if no shot should be taken, and the locks are to be let down to the half bent, it must be studiously kept in mind which is to be let down first, otherwise a barrel is instantly fired without intention. On the construction by which both go off at once I shall make no comment.

From

From the practice of drawing the hinder trigger first, when birds are wild, and a second shot seldom to be had, I have seen persons shoot for several days together without firing the right-hand barrel. By this means it is evident that one barrel and lock will be worn out before the other. When only one half of a gun is thus brought into use, there seems no compensation for the extra weight; and surely a single barrelled gun with a reasonably larger charge would make a better figure. Indeed if your dogs are broke to lie down, till you have reloaded, more shots may be frequently got with a single than, where they are permitted to run in, with a double gun.

Whether the *aim* of a double or single Gun suits your eye best, must be determined by yourself. Though a random sight is more readily caught with the former, there seems a confusion in it from the two muzzles, breeches, and locks, unfavorable to correctness;[13] and it is so different from that of the latter, that whenever you change from one to the other, you will hardly fail to find an inconvenience.

There is indeed a kind of double Gun, known by the name of *Turnabout*,[14] which however little in

[13] I have seldom heard it objected to double guns that the barrels converge at the muzzle so that after a given distance the right hand barrel shoots to the left, and vice versâ. The error is probably not thought of any moment; it may however be worth while to calculate it. Suppose a pair of barrels 2 feet 6 inches long, and of $\frac{6}{10}$ bore; their separation at the breech $\frac{5}{20}$ of an inch, and at the muzzle $\frac{2}{20}$; their axes will cross each other at 11 feet 8 inches from the muzzle, and at 50 yards have diverged so as to be 8 inches $\frac{3}{10}$ asunder, or 4 inches $\frac{3}{20}$ from the line of aim on each side. This deviation may not be noticed in shooting at a sheet of paper, or may be attributed to some other cause; but in cross shots, where the game is in rapid motion, it seems likely to be of real disadvantage, except the nicety of taking a right or left hand shot with its opposite barrel be attended to.

[14] The late Duke of Kingston, of Sporting memory, had a favorite gun, on this construction, made by Bailes; who, if I mis-

in use at present, has the following advantages[15] over that which is in fashion.

As mistake not, was the inventor of the *Iron Rib*, first introduced blue mounting and springs, and left the tints produced by case-hardening on the lock. It is unnecessary to point out the beauty of these tints, or the facility with which the work is kept clean, from the pellicle which is most highly converted into steel, and hardest, being retained on the surface; but many of the workmen themselves, though for fashion sake they put the blue colour on their springs, are ignorant of the advantage arising from it; and that watch springs, after being hardened and tempered, by polishing lose their elasticity, which is restored by blueing. (See Horne's Essay on iron and steel).

I have seen the precious brown of the barrel, and variegated tints of the lock, by the officiousness of a valet, scoured down with emery to the brightness of Martinus Scriblerus's shield, to the horror of the Sportsman, who on the preceding day had been exulting in the beauty of his new gun.

[15] It must be objected to this construction that the Joint on which the barrels turn is apt to become ricketty. Care must also be taken to raise the cock before the barrels are turned round, otherwise the flint will cut them; but this is easily obviated by a regular habit of raising the cock immediately on taking the discharged gun from the shoulder.

As there is no lock to be reached on the left side, there can be no plea for weakening the breech by contracting its width.

There being only one trigger, no mistake can arise from it.

The aim being the same as with a single Gun, no inconvenience can arise in changing occasionally from one to the other.

The discharged barrel being regularly turned below the other, the two are equally used; as are also the hammers.

Those who never cock their Gun till they raise it to the shoulder, cannot be guilty of loading with a lock cocked.

A few guns have been made with one barrel over the other, and a lock on each side; the left pan being sunk to such a depth as to reach the touch-hole of the lower barrel, which in consequence of the prime having to burn so far downward always hangs fire. An improvement on this construction is a desideratum in gun-work.

The

The muzzle of the barrel to be loaded being always uppermost as the butt is on the ground, there is less probability of a charge being put into the wrong barrel; which in loading hastily sometimes happens; and I cannot but think that Guns have actually been burst from this mistake remaining undiscovered: all the blame being unjustly laid on the maker.

If, however, you should not be discouraged by the hazards which I have pointed out, the weight, and two-fold expence of a *double Gun*, and its invidious name, in case you should be reported to have trespassed on your neighbour with one in your hand, I shall give you a few hints on the management of it; concluding with some more general cautions.[16]

[16] On entering a field take observation of all objects to be avoided, that in case of game crossing, or whirling round, your gun may not be fired so as to strike man or cattle.

If you have discharged only one barrel, and are reloading it, before you return the rammer be careful to secure the wadding of the unfired barrel, which from the recoil usually becomes loose. This is not only necessary, lest the shot should fall out, but for safety, as in case of a space between the shot and wadding, the sudden resistance which the shot would meet with, on striking the wadding, might endanger the barrel. I know an instance of a hand being injured a few years since by a Gun bursting, as it was judged, from this cause alone; for one barrel had been fired several times in succession, and this precaution had

> Be not ambitious of displaying your skill by firing close to your companion's head,—or even your favourite pointer's. I have heard of two men shooting together, when one of them, in a show off of this kind, put several shot into his companion's arm, who made suitable lamentations. In the course of the day the wounded man returned the compliment with interest.—" You're " a pretty fellow (cried the man last hit) to make such a piece of " work about my shooting you; why d—mme you've put half " your charge into my leg." " Very likely, (replied the other, " coolly,) but I *killed* my bird, and you *missed* yours."

not been taken with the other; which burst on the first discharge.

Whether you ram the unfired barrel before or after you have shotted the other, adopt one regular time for the operation, lest it should be entirely omitted. If you leave the rammer in the unfired barrel till you have poured shot into the other, be careful that none of it falls into that which holds the rammer, as it may jam, so as to give you considerable trouble.

If birds rise together, and near the shooter, it is not uncommon to see him spoil one, with the first barrel, that another may be shot at a proper distance; and if the first is shot well, the second has frequently got so far as to be only wounded, or missed [17]. If there is a very small interval between the

---

[17] In shooting *alone* with the double Gun, it frequently happens that the attention is taken up by a wounded bird, and the opportunity of a second Shot is neglected; or, on a second bird being shot at, the first is lost, though, if attended to, it might have been

the time of their rising, the *Turnabout* will answer your purpose as well as the common double Gun; and I have shewn that it has some advantages over it.

Let me strictly enjoin you to forbear cocking your Gun till you are actually raising it to the shoulder. Be assured that it is perfectly unnecessary; and that if you are even in expectation of a rabbit crossing a narrow path before you, no advantage will be gained by it. But if there should be any, a little reflection will convince you, that is too dearly purchased by a practice which has given rise to so many accidents. I have a pleasure in considering that I have not only trained young sportsmen in the right way, but have reclaimed even old offenders from this dangerous habit.

I have seen a Gun fired unintentionally by aukwardness in letting down the cock from the

been easily retrieved. The *marker* to a double Gun, should keep his eye on the *first* bird, if wounded, and leave the *second* to the *shooter* himself.

whole

whole to the half bent. To avoid this, be careful not to remove your thumb from the cock till after having let it pass beyond the half bent, and gently raised it again, you hear the sound of the sear catching the tumbler. [18]

On account of Guns being usually carried in the field with the muzzle pointed to the left, and the execrable practice of keeping them cocked, If you have occasion to shoot with a stranger, I shall advise you to plead for the right-hand station, that you cannot hit a bird flying to the left. With a game-keeper take the right-hand without ceremony. In getting over a fence, except you are well assured of your new companion's care, it will

---

[18] Though this practice may be almost general, I must observe that the propriety of it is not self evident, and that it has usually been taught by one Sportsman to another. If not attended to, there is a hazard that the nose of the sear, instead of being secured in the proper notch of the tumbler, should merely bear upon the edge of that notch, and be liable to be shaken off by a slight concussion. It is hardly to be doubted that Guns have unexpectedly gone off, from this circumstance being either unknown, or unattended to.

be safer to compliment him with the honour of preceding you; (an honour which, by the bye, in a thick blackthorn hedge, it may require some little speechifying to force upon his modesty,) you will otherwise frequently find, that while you were passing the hedge, his Gun—cocked—had kept guard—with good aim at your back;—and except you file off as soon as you are clear, the same aim will be kept up till he is clear of the hedge likewise. Should you remonstrate, the usual answer is, *My dear Sir, I assure you, I am remarkably careful.*

Should he appear to consider a cocked Gun as the best tool to beat bushes with, tell him you are too nervous to touch a feather in company, and get out of shot as fast as you can.

When you cross a ditch be upon your guard, that in case of falling your muzzle may be immediately directed upwards. Few persons indeed have sufficient practice in falling to bring this to a regular habit, but remember that you *may* fall.

If

If you should think it necessary to put your Gun into any attendant's hands, either for a time, or to be carried home, let me recommend to you to secure the flint or hammer by some sort of case, which any man may invent and make of leather himself; or go a step farther, and draw the charge. I do not approve of shaking out the priming; in which case the Gun will be considered us unloaded, (except that the hammer is put into, and left in, the barrel,) and it is a fact, that Guns have been fired when no priming has appeared in the pan [19].

I shall

---

[19] It will be sufficient to illustrate this by the two following anecdotes. A Servant at Grange, (the Seat of J. Lister Kaye, Esq.) going into his master's room, and seeing a Gun *unprimed, therefore supposed to be unloaded*, aimed it at a portrait; snapping the lock, as though he would say "here I have you, and there I have you;" when on the third pull of the trigger, the Gun went off, and gave such a finishing touch to the canvas, as the Painter himself had little foreseen.

But a more serious case was communicated to me by the Rev. Dr. Goodenough, in whose Grandfather's house the misfortune happened, many years since, at Broughton in Oxfordshire. A young lady, about thirteen, then on a visit, came into the room where a party was sitting at cards, with a small Gun, (which had been laid by with the

I shall here point out a source of danger to which you are exposed, from the charge of powder which you are in the act of pouring into the barrel being inflamed, either by tow left in it after cleaning, or a part of the wadding remaining on fire within. I can hardly suppose this to have happened where card-wadding was used;[20] it may from paper; but tow

the hammer up, and the priming shaken out,) crying "I'll shoot you," and pointing it at several persons present. She soon found out how to manage the lock, and Dr. G.'s father remonstrating with her she snapped it at him above twenty times, and became so troublesome that her own maid was sent for to take the Gun from her. The giddy little girl retired into a corner, threatening, and continued to snap the lock very dextrously, when in a struggle the Gun went off, and killed the unfortunate maid on the spot!

It seems probable that in both these cases, the concussion of the lock had loosened the powder which lay in the touch-hole, so that it fell gradually into the pan. In the former instance the Gun had been newly charged, and the powder was readily disengaged; in the latter with greater difficulty. But any person may satisfy himself by a few trials, that the sparks will frequently catch dry powder, lying in the touch-hole, notwithstanding that there shall not be a single grain in the pan.

[20] Most persons who use stamped wadding, have found this inconvenience, that in attempting to draw it, the worm of the rammer

tow seems more hazardous. In some instances the charge alone has been inflamed, the top of the flask having been removed in time, or the slider preventing communication with its contents. But it has happened that the whole flask has been blown up; and not many months since in the case of a gentleman in a northern county, attended with the loss of sight.[21] This hazard is easily obviated, by any method

---

rammer frequently slips, so as to turn the wadding edgewise; and if over the powder, in a chambered breech, it becomes necessary to blow it out. This is most simply obviated by screwing the worm, for a turn or two, through the center of a piece of fresh wadding, before the rammer is introduced into the barrel. By this process you have a guide to the *center* of what you wish to draw, and will seldom fail to secure it on the first trial.

[21] The following are the circumstances of the unfortunate accident by which Sir John Swinburne, Bart. was a sufferer in March 1799.

His Gun was single barrelled, with a patent antichambered breech. The flask copper, with a spring charger, and at that time contained nearly a pound of Gunpowder.

Having flashed off at the door of his house he proceeded to the dog-kennel, and he thinks that at least five minutes must have elapsed

method of detaching the measured charge of powder

elapsed before he began to load. Having primed he poured the charge, cut off by the slider, into the barrell, when the whole contents of the Flask instantly exploded ! A large piece of copper struck the right eye, and injured the bone above, so that it has continued to exfoliate till within a few weeks of this time, (April 1801.) The lock remained at half bent, and it cannot be doubted that some *tow*, which had been left in the barrel, or chamber, continuing on fire from the time of flashing off, was the occasion of this misfortune.

In every instance (excepting one) of which I have been able to ascertain the particulars, among the numerous accidents of this kind which have lately been communicated to me, the explosion has happened on the second time of powder being poured into the the barrel on that day, which is strong evidence of the cause above suggested. If the accident has become more frequent within these few years, it must be attributed to the general use of *chambered breech plugs*, in which detached particles of tow are so likely to be lodged. But lest I should be thought to lay any stress on this as an objection to them, I shall produce much better authority than my own in favor of their principle, in an extract from *Count Rumford's* Experiments on Gunpowder; one important conclusion from which he has expressed thus,——
" The most simple and most effectual manner of accelerating the inflammation and combustion of Gunpowder would, in my opinion

der from the flask, before it is poured into the barrel.[22]

In drying gunpowder, be careful to separate from your magazine, of whatever kind, the mere quantity which you wish to dry at once; suppose five or six charges; thus, in case of an accident, you may escape, like myself, with burnt eyebrows and eyelashes;—but should you pour into a shovel, unfortunately over-heated, from your stock, even

opinion, be to set fire to the charge of powder by shooting, through a small opening, the flame of a smaller charge into the midst of it." (Phil. Trans. for 1797, page 285.)

It must be remarked that this clear description of Mr. Nock's patent Gun breech was not intentional, though standing as a proof that those who reason and experiment well on the same subject come to the same conclusions. The opinion of our best Gunmakers may be collected from their practice in adopting the principle of the chambered plugs, however, for special reasons, they have modified their form.

[22] That vulgar implement, a tobacco pipe bowl, has perhaps more merit than Sportsmen of a higher class allow to it.

of a single pound, however *cerebri felicem*, nothing will save you.[23]

I remember your laughing at my hyper-caution, when handling various Guns in the maker's shop, I shifted the muzzles so that at no one instant any one was pointed at a limb of the several persons around us. I was not then exerting any particular care; the practice was habitual to me; and I wish to impress upon your mind, that with respect to the muzzle being suffered, during the fraction of a second, to point towards any human being, *a Gun should always be considered as loaded.* How have the numerous accidents happened from the kitchen wit of terrifying the maids, by threatening to shoot them, but in presuming Guns not to be

[23] Gunpowder may be safely dried in an iron pan, kept bright, for as iron does not change colour by a heat below 430°. Farenheit, nor Gunpowder explode at less than about 550°. at which the iron will have acquired a deep violet tint, this test will answer every purpose of Security. By suffering a slight tinge to come upon your pan before you take it from the fire, and strew your powder in it, you may apply a heat twice as great as that of boiling water; but to keep within that which produces colour on the iron would be more satisfactory.

loaded?

loaded? In some of these cases the trigger has been drawn unintentionally;—in others, with a view to study the passion of terror in the human countenance, (inexcusable thus, even in a painter) by snapping the lock;—sometimes in a struggle from persons interfering.[24] This spieces of frolic, I fear, has not been totally confined to the kitchen;— but on this head I chuse to be silent.

I have not written thus to deter you from a captivating amusement, but to enable you to enjoy it with greater security. Many of your friends could have told you all that I have done, and much more; but till they shall take the trouble to do it, neglect not what I have intended for your advantage.

[24] See the second accident in Note 19.

FINIS.

Smeeton, Printer, St. Martin's Lane.